How Long Has This Apocalypse Been Going On

poems by

Laura Z. Fairgrieve

Finishing Line Press
Georgetown, Kentucky

How Long Has This Apocalypse Been Going On

ACKNOWLEDGMENTS

Thankful acknowledgment is made to the editors of all publications in which
the following poems originally appeared:

Mortar Magazine: Drifting towards Refuge
Mortar Magazine: This is how the house falls down

Publisher: Leah Huete de Maines
Editor: Christen Kincaid
Cover Art: Laura Z. Fairgrieve
Author Photo: Laura Z. Fairgrieve
Cover Design: Elizabeth Maines McCleavy

Order online: www.finishinglinepress.com
also available on amazon.com

Author inquiries and mail orders:
Finishing Line Press
PO Box 1626
Georgetown, Kentucky 40324
USA

Contents

"*I was pretending that I did not speak their language; on the moon we spoke a soft, liquid tongue, and sang in the starlight, looking down on the dead dried world.*"

—Shirley Jackson, *We Have Always Lived in the Castle*

Pandemic dream

I'm falling asleep on the train
and the sky is swallowing
                      itself again

a shroud or a ceiling unfolds
opaque as the snake jumps off
                         its track
again, dark overhead
                  merging
into murkiness
and the train cartwheeling into
                     a coil
is suddenly upside
-down
but rattling less

a frictionless nothing
that pants in my ear,
that stares back out of
the window that I cannot see

my daughter counts 100 cheerios
on the 100th day of school
from her sealed bedroom,
when she holds them up to the screen
her teacher thinks they are dead insects,
                     dried out
little husks
daughter so proud,
                       always counting
numbering us into circuits
loop
                after loop

another night's breath
            rattles the walls

up and ahead
eyes windowed
and Mars is findable but

it has been nearly four years
since I have seen any stars

Drifting towards Refuge

"No one leaves home unless home is the mouth of a shark."
—*Warsan Shire*

When you hack your breath into a hot air balloon
Make sure that the canvas is dyed dark for the nighttime
Splash it solid and forget the careful batiks from your living room floor

When you row through the transatlantic gusts that are salty-sharp
    and new
Pretend that it is a breeze on the Queiq, hushing you with its smell of
    mother's hands
Like dough and dried flowers, like the hope of rain

When a fresh darkness is kicked up and claws its way through a
    seamless escape
Thrust your oar through the westward air,
gather into your arms the artillery of a quiet night
and push yourself into the zephyr, into the splinters
ahead, the promise of nothing.

Borders

In the west we spell border like murder
we kick the door shut and solder its hinges
so that only the ghosts can slip through
Border
from the Old French word *bord*, or a ship's edge
that we cannot help casting bodies over
(it wouldn't be our first live burial at sea)
why board when we can bord, carve a line
like a dare and pretend it is electric
Now really make it electric
and see whose bones we can
gather beneath.

Sketching Maps

Lines, oceans.
This time

the matrices twist
into something

breathless.
They are knitting

continents
out of rotations.

Each spin
suffers something

new
Kicks up

the wrong wave
Elbows a dove

out of
orbit.

This speed is
natural but

Each turn
is thoughtless

Hunts degree
after degree

with so much
exactitude

It aches

Quarantine

I need this to be known—I was never
the only one

The windows did not lead outside
and threats built walls
of invisible teeth

Where
were you when my
family became a maze

when the barriers grew from our breath
into plexiglass between our faces

Please
shovel some snow over here
just so I have something to lay with

unhinge the temperature
to a slaughter degree

I am reading my astrology chart
just for something to take it out on

I'm looking for a door to slam
at the bottom of a well

Pandemic Ubi Sunt

a teacher in Brooklyn
is projected to the front
of the classroom by the
keening wishes of

thirty ten-year-olds
she waves a foggy hand
she is particles
            of light
dipping and burning
she is gone but still smiling, wherever she is
where ever gone leads

Multi-generational houses
are shrunk down to a single strand
unspooling into memory as
winter bore down
straight through the bone
and only left discarded
                        longings
and   names

Names and negative
                        spaces

Each name feels like

Fingernails growing backwards

Swallowing an ocean

Or a spoonful of dread

Now our dreams are a series

of empty rooms

Right now I am putting a curse on the Vessel

I need a witness to this—
I hate the Vessel.

      I am speaking against the Vessel
with all of my air.

      I have walked it before.
It feels like I am pacing the bloodstream
      of someone who'd rather be empty.
Or maybe I am confusing my own
      longing for emptiness,
the tickling finger of nothingness
      that taunts on all sides,
but no one is walking the right speed
      I feel transparent but I clog the air
I'm knit into this web of sweat—
      that's nothing new
and the only thing that I can say
      about the suicides
is that I am tangling this badly.

      I don't know anything
about any of it
      or how things were for you, all of you
but
I could not keep it to myself
I could not keep my mouth shut
When a curse means
I miss you

Post-Contact

Before the hurt could think to have a name
it bubbled out of a puddle turning
into a swamp—now a lake—one with jaws.
It was wide and gaping and wanted to consume
anything
all of it

while the floodwaters coursed into the house
through secret channels like mice in winter
(those basements not meant to be lived in)
while the South doubled over in the snap
and Washington, Canada roasted alive
the neighbors fought so loud about exposure
that the streets started to tremble
and couldn't catch their breath

the window was open
the butterflies looked drunk,
but that could have been
our jealousy talking

They traveled so far

They hovered so close together
and our bodies busy brewed some
cold fever inside us,
a slow shock beyond contact
that settled in for the years

Still-life of Washington D. C.

Leaves scratch the window
vinegar woven into the air like
an old hooked rug
but this time
something impatient

a memo released
on the fingers of noon
a half-drunk paper cup
that is forgetting how
to hold itself together
with coffee stretching out
like a shadow, or tar

business as usual until
the ground feels wrong
the air looks tired
smells like an excuse
molecules of oxygen getting
shaky, hiding in desk drawers
and at the corners of things

a great gust comes
and it trips over itself
on its way to snuff out
what looks like the sun

Earth Cradle

I just want to hold the earth in my arms
push her wet face against my chest, tell her
Shhhh baby, I know it hurts
my bindings are threaded for fight or flight
and I can't remember how we got here either
but the tire tracks don't lie
I want to cradle her like a soft newborn
blow on her fever wild forehead
tell her
Shhhh we know who made us this way
hold her close, tell her that we don't owe
them forgiveness

The Earth and the Air might still draw breath or a bath

A teenage girl paints fractals on her eyelids
and holds her child back from the open window
six stories up and the sky is a wet parachute
waiting to kiss the dirt.

Aid workers or someone's cousins
mine the cadavers of houses
for whispers of something green
and the hope of Daddy still speaking.

The clouds choke the wind
they fork and somersault around
four armed drones
four eyed phantoms with
puppet strings spanning the globe
and rockets spring from next door
like string lights in the summer.

The twins take a bath
in a clawfoot porcelain tub
that is the lone island in a
shell of rubble and stunted columns
holding up no ceiling
rain falls onto their heads and feels
like fingertips smoothing their hair.
They make braids for each other
the ruins melt into mosaic tiles
and it could almost be anywhere.

The skies cannot be trusted, but
neither can the walls
the heart of the city is silent in
its chest cavity, it is pillowed by promises
that are nothing but fog,
and when the wind coughs and
the clouds shuffle
this could be anywhere.

Song for the Living

survival slides down my throat
like the cold yolk of an egg at night
when the sun has disappeared
and all sounds muffled
are still more desperate.

imagine that love is all it takes
to make it all still beating, still
gliding through potential and possibility
when all along there is a metallic thrum
of chaos coloring every
minute alive.

A Study of Lunar Research Flights

*"The cost to science of destroying the pristine lunar
environment did not seem of concern to our sponsors—but
it certainly was to us, as I made clear at the time."*
—Leonard Rieffel

Sketch out the circumference of the moon
Chart her curves, break down
her substances
Send the moon something nice to wear
a bouquet of stilted breath
For her date
with detonation

When we release the bomb
Will her dust bloom into
White lilies
Will the gases turn her heart
Inside out

Whatever happens is probably worth it
The moon is used to playing second fiddle
She is becoming too vain from all
of the photos we take anyway
Burn her skin off and see what's underneath
Expose her or ruin her, either way
Give her a purpose
Give us something worth seeing.

Post-Trauma

After it all, I am still the child scolded in public,
the girl pulling off her scabs, wishing on them like dandelions
and pining after the same temporary high
of sharp anima or a compliment. After
all the broken fingers and extinguished moonlight
the cloudy edifice of my body is still reluctant
to be named, still clings to the same chill in the daytime.

I am always staring down from the edge of things,
wondering if this is the drop that will finally collapse
me, that will disassemble me in a firestorm instead
of a fog, past all familiar hurts and remembered afflictions,
and into smoothness—blank and new, not mine.

The End

Sing to us of a rage not above
but around and within
A road paved with wasps and
bricked with forgettings

Sing us to quiet, to what waits behind sleep.

I.
The fire fled the match
and the split ends of everyone's hair
smelled like burning, smelled like
ashes falling from the sky like pigeons.

The trains rocketed past with
their doors hanging open and
the headphones, the Marvel lunchbox,
somebody's tomato soup and somebody's
Grandma colored the tunnel wall red.

The kids faraway signed up for war
and the wars nearby spent all their
ammo on the kids in school
and still the drones leapt upwards
like bats from a cave, and the bullets sang.

II.
Our hands are whispers of smoke
and our eyes are overcast
we throw knives at the sky
and forget about her pockmarks.
We dream of erasing the moon.

III.
The river is on fire and the fish
think that the sun has given up
the world underneath is not murky—
it is choking.

The poles curl into the fetal position
they are shrinking and the oceans
chew at their corners, not knowing
any better.

IV.
Our hearts are empty museums now
cataloging the lost and the dead
with accuracy that turns into souvenir
the more time we spend with it.

How Long Has this Apocalypse Been Going On

Try me. Look at me wrong and I'll spit
a hundred roses into a bucket
I'll nurse my ribboned tongue into
stitches and forget all edges

Cough up. I'm drinking down everything
stagnant and spinning myself like
a jewelry box ballerina tethered
to a grave, blanketed in stamens
how long will this ailing
melody continue to groan

Look long. The levees will explode
into a fountain and the disturbed
mosquitoes will marshal themselves
into a choir for an unfamiliar throng

We're past magnitude. Now I'm
throwing fistfuls of coins at a metric
ton of fossils, no sounds echo, no
stunning hits, no needling loose, no
dances, no ruins, no thorns, no
wounds or words, no
not even
a hope of shattering

There is no synonym for pandemic

To be here now is
To feel or express
To grieve or lament
To show the usual
   signs

what are the usual   signs
when a million and climbing
have been   disappeared
fridged, flowered, buried
and the globe   even sicker

how to act   when
structure has broken its
feet
buried its head
in the mud

when the collective is
frowning in   smithereens
and the neighbors are having
a tea party with the pigeons
on the fire escape
now I want to be   a   pigeon
now I want to be   fire
without an escape
I want all the walls
To be   here   now
to feel themselves burn
cave, crumble, shout
each alone and dying
   now

I want all the pigeons
To be here now
to hurl and to haunt
loose from their flocks
To be here now

is to
be on the wrong side
of the   window
is laying down to   breathe
through the   crack   under

the door
is to
fake it and believe it
is to
shiver in summer
is to
watch the days somersault
into   new   seasons
is to count   quiet   shadows
is to watch and wait
is to soon   forget
how to count
To be here now
is to be here, to mouth silent
words, to   breathe and to   mourn

This is how the house falls down

With forty-five spectators and a bucket of ash
With little boys blowing it kisses like rockets
With rubble like chalk dust coating everyone's faces
With no way to know which direction that pillar will fall in
With twelve newborn kittens directly in its path
With the snapped necks of plumbing spinning like sprinklers
With spoiled cartons of milk tumbling out of the fridge
With the fish tank starting an electrical fire
And the boys blowing kisses, and the boys blowing kisses
And the foundation still gasping,
swallows them whole.

Night Song

Sleep, this isn't all there is
Tuck in the corners of any nightmare
and exhale a gentle shield

Remember your mouth can work both ways
Speak, you remember
the battering rams are trotting
home to pasture

Unwrap your throat, peel off the
packing paper and gut the masking tape
Love, this is not all there is
the seed has shed its shell now.

Laura received her MFA from Adelphi University. She is a winner of the *Poets & Writers* Amy Award. Her poems appear in the anthology *Women of Resistance: Poems for a New Feminism* published by O/R Books. Her work has appeared in *Arkana Magazine, The Banyan Review, Permafrost Magazine, Lines + Stars, The Bitchin' Kitsch, Mortar Magazine,* and *Ink in Thirds,* among others.

www.ingramcontent.com/pod-product-compliance
Lightning Source LLC
Chambersburg PA
CBHW022105080426
42734CB00009B/1492